Women Who Rock

MALALA YOUSAFZAI

GAIL TERP

WORLD BOOK

BOLT

This World Book edition of *Malala Yousafzai*
is published by agreement between
Black Rabbit Books and World Book, Inc.
© 2017 Black Rabbit Books,
2140 Howard Dr. West,
North Mankato, MN 56003 U.S.A.
World Book, Inc.,
180 North LaSalle St., Suite 900,
Chicago, IL 60601 U.S.A.

Design and Production by Michael Sellner
Photo Research by Rhonda Milbrett

Library of Congress Control Number: 2015954928

HC ISBN: 978-0-7166-9461-8   PB ISBN: 978-0-7166-9462-5

Printed in the United States at CG Book Printers,
North Mankato, Minnesota, 56003. PO #1799 4/16

Contents

CHAPTER 1

Mighty Words

Malala Yousafzai stood before the crowd. She was small, but she was mighty. When she began to speak, the crowd listened. She spoke with power and humor. She told the crowd about the need for schools worldwide. She said girls and boys have a right to be educated.

A Powerful Activist

Yousafzai is known for fighting for education. In fact, she was shot because of her work.

Yousafzai grew up in **Pakistan**. A group called the **Taliban** was in charge where she lived. The Taliban said girls couldn't go to school. Yousafzai spoke against the rules. The Taliban sent a gunman to shoot her. But she survived, and she still stands up for education.

HER OWN WORDS

❝... my brothers still call me that annoying bossy sister. As far as I know, I am just a committed and even stubborn person who wants to see every child getting quality education ...❞

Fun Facts

has received more than 40 awards and honors

HER NAME MEANS "GRIEF STRICKEN."

SPEAKS 3 LANGUAGES

6'
5'
4'

HAS AN ASTEROID
NAMED AFTER HER

SPOKE TO THE
UNITED NATIONS
ON HER
16TH BIRTHDAY

5 feet
(1.5 m)
tall

3'

2'

1'

0

CHAPTER 2

Early
Life

Yousafzai was born July 12, 1997. When she was born, her parents cheered. But their neighbors did not. At that time, most parents in Pakistan thought girls were not important. Yousafzai's parents did not agree. They were happy with her birth.

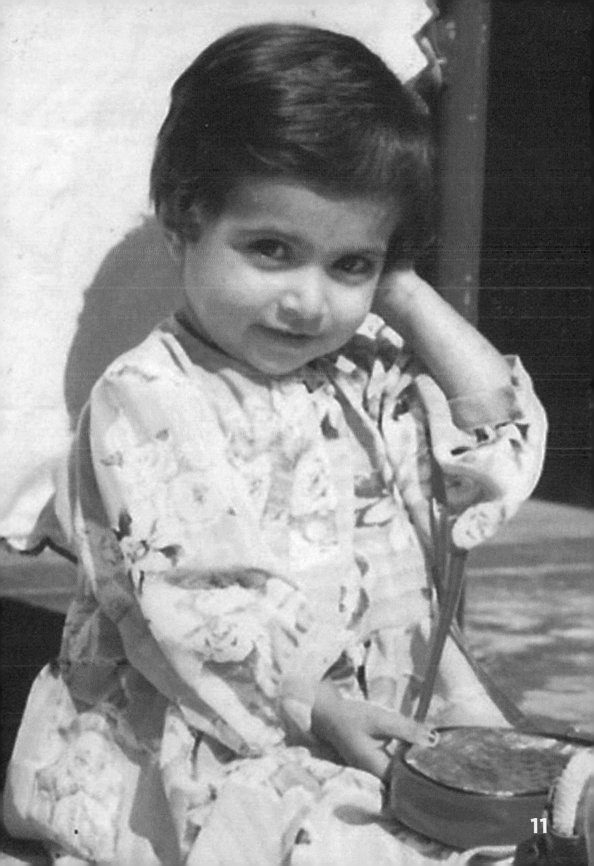

Pakistan by the Numbers

67.39
number of • • • •
years an
average
Pakistani
lives

45.8
percent of
women can
read and write

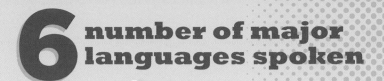

6 number of major
languages spoken

199,085,847
number of people
who live there

307,374
square miles
(796,095 square kilometers)
country's size

13

Going to School

Yousafzai grew up in a place called Swat Valley. Most girls in Swat didn't go to school. Yousafzai's father thought this was wrong. He opened a school for both boys and girls. Yousafzai and her two brothers went to school there.

Yousafzai was a great student.

The Blog

When Yousafzai was 10, her life changed. The Taliban moved into Swat Valley. They used guns to make people follow their rules. They blew up schools that allowed girls. In 2009, Yousafzai began to write a **blog**. She wrote about how girls should be able to go to school. The blog quickly became popular.

Yousafzai used a different name on the blog. She called herself Gul Makai.

CHAPTER 3

Big Changes

The Taliban grew stronger. The Pakistani army fought the Taliban. The fighting was terrible. In May 2009, the Yousafzais had to leave Swat Valley. Many others left too.

Three months later, the Yousafzais returned home. They were happy to be back. But the Taliban was still a problem. Yousafzai began to give speeches. She spoke out against the Taliban. She pushed for more girls' schools.

Percent of People Who Can Read and Write

World	Pakistan	United States	Canada
85%	57.9%	99%	99%

100
75
50
25
0

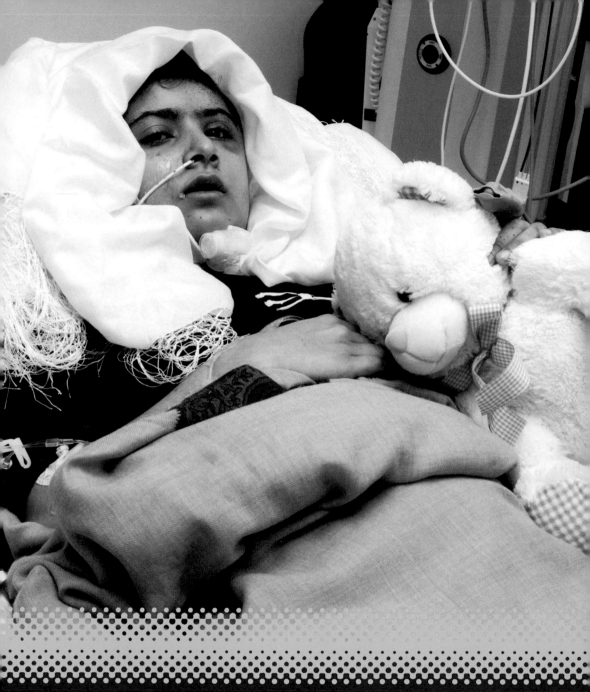

Two other girls were also shot.
However, they were not as badly hurt.

The Shooting

On October 9, 2012, Yousafzai sat on a school bus. As she talked with friends, a man stopped the bus. He said, "Who is Malala?" None of the girls spoke. But some looked at Yousafzai. The man pointed a gun and shot her in the head. She was hurt badly.

Yousafzai's brain **swelled**. Doctors didn't know if she would live. But after many months, she healed. And she was ready to speak out again.

CHAPTER 4

Yousafzai Today

News of the shooting spread around the world. Yousafzai became famous. People called her the girl who fought for the right to learn.

In 2013, she spoke at the United Nations. In her speech, she spoke of the Taliban.

HER OWN WORDS

"They thought that the bullet would silence us. But they failed."

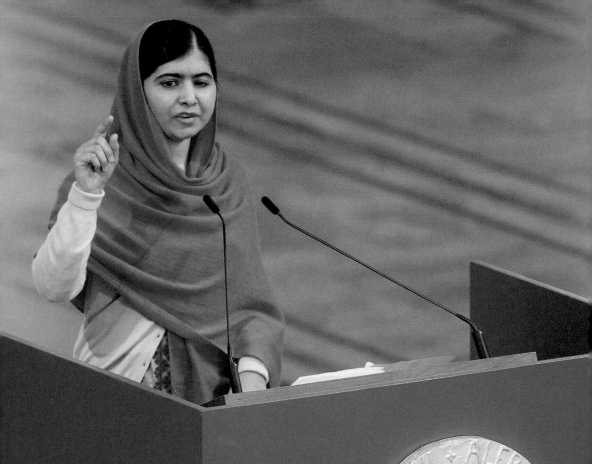

AGE RANGE OF NOBEL PEACE PRIZE WINNERS

oldest (Joseph Rotblat)
average age
youngest (Malala Yousafzai)

ages

Nobel Peace Prize

Yousafzai received the Nobel Peace Prize in 2014. This prize **honors** people who work for peace. She is the youngest person to receive it.

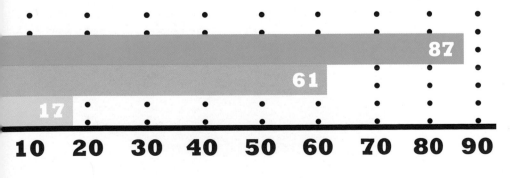

In the Spotlight

Yousafzai continues to bring education to all children. She opened a school in Syria. She also formed the Malala Fund. This group raises money to **improve** education for girls.

No one can doubt Yousafzai is a powerful voice. She's likely to stay in the spotlight for many years.

Telling Her Story

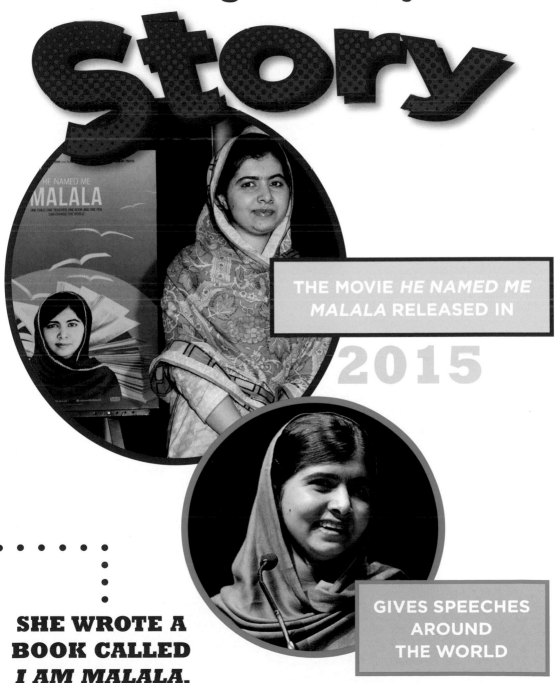

Story

THE MOVIE *HE NAMED ME MALALA* RELEASED IN

2015

SHE WROTE A BOOK CALLED *I AM MALALA.*

GIVES SPEECHES AROUND THE WORLD

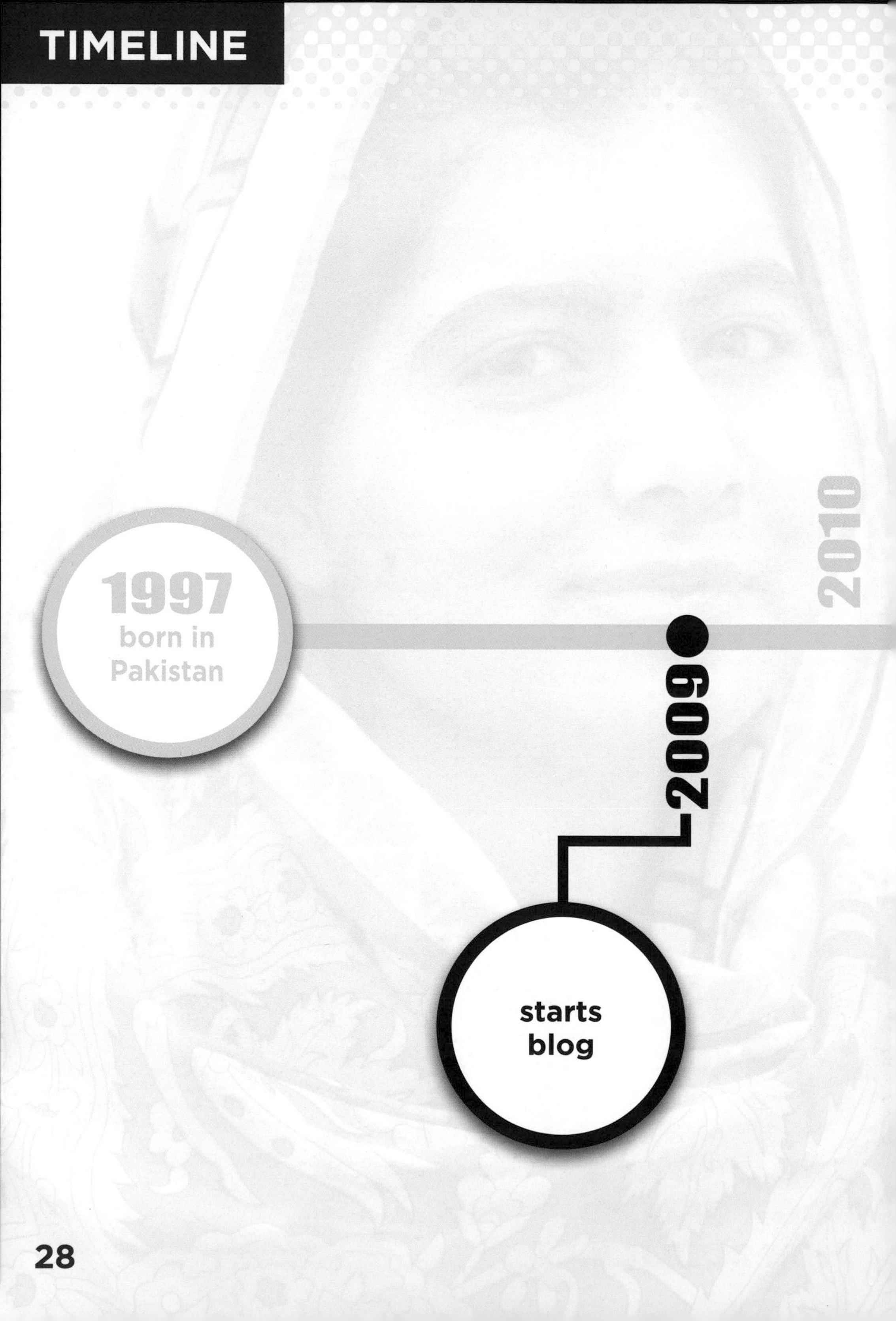

1997
born in
Pakistan

2009

2010

starts
blog

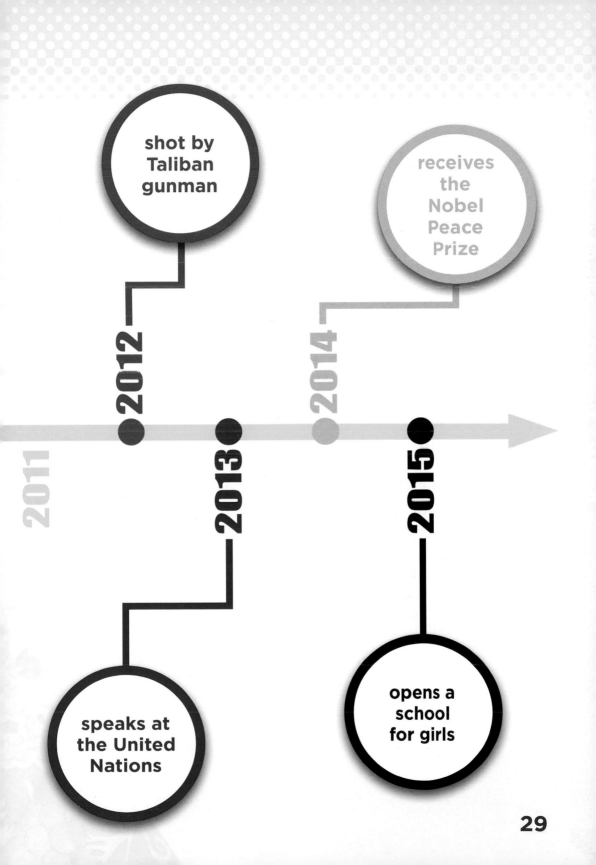

shot by Taliban gunman

receives the Nobel Peace Prize

2012

2014

2011

2013

2015

speaks at the United Nations

opens a school for girls

GLOSSARY

asteroid (AS-tuh-royd)—a large space rock that moves around the Sun

blog (BLAHG)—an online journal

honor (AH-ner)—an award or respect for someone

improve (im-PROOV)—to make something better

Pakistan (PAK-uh-stan)—a country in southern Asia

swell (SWEL)—to become larger than normal

Taliban (TAHL-uh-ban)—a terrorist group that uses violence to control others

United Nations (YOO-ny-ted NAY-shuns)—an organization of 193 countries that works for world peace

BOOKS

Barker, Geoff. *Discover Pakistan. Discover Countries.* New York: PowerKids Press, 2012.

Doak, Robin S. *Malala Yousafzai. A True Book.* New York: Children's Press, 2015.

McCarney, Rosemary A., and Plan International. *Dear Malala, We Stand with You.* New York: Crown Books for Young Readers, 2015.

WEBSITES

The Geography of Pakistan
www.ducksters.com/geography/country/ pakistan.php

Malala Yousafzai
www.biography.com/people/ malala-yousafzai-21362253#after-the-attack

Pakistan
www.timeforkids.com/destination/pakistan

INDEX